WHAT'S
IN THE
BLOOD

To Fred

Meander in

Grace

Cheryl

THE DREAMSEEKER
POETRY SERIES

Books in the DreamSeeker Poetry Series, intended to make available fine writing by Anabaptist-related poets, are published by Cascadia Publishing House under the DreamSeeker Books imprint and often copublished with Herald Press. Cascadia oversees content of these poetry collections in collaboration with the DreamSeeker Poetry Series Editor Jeff Gundy (Jean Janzen volumes 1-4) as well as in consultation with its Editorial Council and the authors themselves.

Also worth noting are two poetry collections that would likely have been included in the series had it been in existence then:

1. Empty Room with Light
   By Ann Hostetler, 2002
2. A Liturgy for Stones
   By David Wright, 2003

WHAT'S IN THE BLOOD

POEMS BY
CHERYL DENISE

<u>DreamSeeker Poetry Series, Volume 9</u>

DreamSeeker Books
TELFORD, PENNSYLVANIA

an imprint of
Cascadia Publishing House LLC

Cascadia Publishing House orders, information, reprint permissions:
contact@CascadiaPublishingHouse.com
1-215-723-9125
126 Klingerman Road, Telford PA 18969
www.CascadiaPublishingHouse.com

What's in the Blood
Copyright © 2012 by Cascadia Publishing House,
Telford, PA 18969
All rights reserved
DreamSeeker Books is an imprint of Cascadia Publishing House LLC
Library of Congress Catalog Number: 2010017657
ISBN 13: 978-1-931038-92-8; ISBN 10: 1-931038-92-9
Book design by Cascadia Publishing House
Cover design by Gwen M. Stamm
Cover art by Kenneth Kreider, www.artwv.com

The paper used in this publication is recycled and meets the
minimum requirements of American National Standard for Information
Sciences—Permanence of Paper for Printed Library Materials, ANSI Z39.48-1984.1984

Versions of poems in this collection have appeared in various outlets as
listed in Credits page.

Library of Congress Cataloguing-in-Publication Data
Denise, Cheryl, 1965-
What's in the blood / Cheryl Denise.
    p. cm. -- (DreamSeeker poetry series ; v. 9)
    Summary: "What's in the Blood offers plainspoken and often humor-
ous poetry that explores the angst of childhood, the earthiness of live-
stock sales, the wonder of Mennonite martyrs, and the tragedy of West
Virginia mine explosions"--Provided by publisher.
    ISBN-13: 978-1-931038-92-8 (trade pbk. : alk. paper)
    ISBN-10: 1-931038-92-9 (trade pbk. : alk. paper)
    I. Title.
PS3604.E585W48 2011
811'.6--dc23
                            2011028272

18 17 16 15 14 13 12   10 9 8 7 6 5 4 3 2 1

For my husband, Mike

Contents

WHAT'S
IN THE
BLOOD

Toil and Grace

Grandma said a lazy Mennonite
doesn't understand his Bible.
Praying can be done while working.

Remnants remain
and my generation still believes,
even while growing richer
and moving to cities,
even though no one dies for the faith
like Dirk Willems or Annekin Hendricks.
We like to think we inherited
those stiff stubborn beliefs,
banished from Zurich and Landau,
fleeing to Philadelphia,
finding farms in Waterloo.

Surely Jesus was joking,
his parable of the vineyard workers,
that the less than industrious
will get into heaven.
He began life as a carpenter,
worked miracles on Sundays,
walked miles, taught multitudes,
looked after his mom while being crucified.

I lay block for old Charlie's foundation,
take Mrs. Gingrich Sunday dinners
mixing mortar, kneading bread.
How else would I know if the baptism took?

We love with our hands,
rebuilding after hurricanes,
piecing quilts for refugees.
We work till we are too tired to sin
(but we sin anyway.)

Sunday mornings we gather to sing
loud, unaccompanied
our hands quiet and still for this hour,
our voices so sure of grace. ✤

Nickel Mines, PA, Oct. 2nd, 2006

In the white-fenced schoolyard,
there in the ball-diamond with the chicken-wire backstop,
a girl runs barefoot around the bases,
her long lavender dress and black apron flying.
Boys in suspenders stomp their disbelief as she crosses
    home.

From the yellow one-room school
Emma Mae pulls the bell rope,
ushers them inside to lessons.
A grinning six-year-old offers her a jar of goldenrod.
While they quietly find their desks, fold their hands:
Our Father who art in Heaven,
a man thunders in
with a gun, knives, chains.
He pulls the shades, orders the boys Out.

Before sunrise the man drove a silver dairy tank
down their dirt lanes and collected milk from their barns
as he had for years.

Now he foretells of torture.
A window shade flaps open.
Go, an angel whispers to a freckled girl.
She escapes while he turns, jerks the white ring of the shade.

He binds ten pairs of feet.
Thirteen-year-old Marian says, *Shoot me first.*
She wants to save the younger ones

she can't. . . .

her classmate in French braids dies
    beneath the blackboard
        white chalk above proclaiming
        Visitors Bring Unexpected Blessings.

He turns the gun on himself.

Amish neighbors go to the gunman's home,
to extend forgiveness,
bringing jars of preserves and raisin pies.

Grandfathers instruct children,
The man is troubled; he is not evil and we must forgive.

Under kerosene lamps
five mothers wash their daughters' bodies,
lift their losses into white dresses,
pin coverings in their downy hair.
Girls pulled from their mothers' wombs, again.

Five pine caskets
lowered into the ground,
black clad fathers shovel the rich, dark dirt.
There is no singing; a hymn is read.

Four a.m., Thursday, a wrecking team
knocks down the bell tower, bulldozes the school.
Men in straw hats watch, shake their heads,
farm-worn hands slack at their sides.

The blood-soaked place shall become a quiet pasture
where the Lord like a Shepherd
     leads his loved ones
          to lie down. ❧

Diminished

Grandma sits in her wheelchair
between bed and window,
her new short hair sticking up on one side.
An aide in cartoon scrubs bounces in, nails painted green,
pats the strayed gray hair and announces,
Here's your peach schnapps, Sweetie,
setting down a plastic cup of orange juice.

I'm pretty sure Grandma doesn't know
what peach schnapps is.
I remember when she started bowling at age seventy,
explaining how it wasn't sinful
since she and her friends bowled in the morning,
and there was no smoking or drinking.

I ask the aide how Grandma's getting along.
Oh we had to beat her last night to get her to behave.
She laughs, winking at Grandma,
who smiles like an uncertain child.

After talk of apple fritters in her old kitchen,
the latest on the great-grandchildren,
I don't know what else to say,
how to connect to where she is now,
so I stoop, hug her good-bye, ask *Do you need anything?*
Just your love, she says.

At the elevator I press the down arrow
and, bewildered, wait
until a nurse comes and punches in the code
that allows me to escape. ✱

Things That Matter

And there they are
outside my kitchen window
in backhoes and blue jeans,
smoking cigarettes at six a.m.
stubborn as cattle
shovels digging trenches in the rain.

While I worry over red marks on my manuscript,
consult dictionary, thesaurus,
crumple poems for the trash,
they lay pipe, pull electric, chug Pepsi,
fix what I did wrong two months ago.
And if there's anything I know now,
it's that you need to lay Schedule 40
to pull electric.
All you need to know in life
is what these men know.

If I were my mother,
I'd serve them sweet tea
and gingersnaps
from a wicker tray.

I wish I'd been born a man.
Old Mrs. Evans said a girl
could hurt something female working like they do.
But most women don't even try,
don't own a proper work shoe,
won't break a sweat outside a gym.

The only thing we're better at
is multiple orgasms,
and that's important
but men figuring, calculating,
getting something done
something real
pulling cable
sliding in and out of days
green as grass
the mist rising
working under whatever the sky will give. ❁

Rejection by Mail

it came last night
and I couldn't even indulge
in a rush of profanity
friends were coming for dinner.

Afterwards I dreamt of a fish
in a puddle I was barricading
when he lunged at me
bit my arm.

In the letter
he said he liked the one about sisters.
It's not my favorite.

My husband says I'll get a book published
it's just a matter of time.
He doesn't want to live with me depressed.

His work is concrete
you can walk in it.
He can do anything, except preach.
He'll repair your roof, in the rain,
if you're somewhat desperate and poor.

Sometimes I feel like my Grandmother
here to serve lemonade
and sweet rolls to strengthen others
so they can do the real work.

And now the stranger I dreamed of loving
has sent a three-paragraphed no.

I want my husband to join me in defaming him
but I've heard he's a likable guy.

His letter is folded in thirds
in my underwear drawer
unsexy as hell. ❀

Economic Development

Clear all topsoil and vegetation,
burn the trees.

Blast the mountaintop
after all maybe God was wrong.

Splinter rock strata,
crack the foundation of Debra Burke's home.

Drive a dragline with the scoop the size
of the devil's mouth, eat the black seam.

Push the burden–heavy chaff
down valleys and streams.

Throw hydro seed like manna;
level land for shopping malls.

Build silos and sludge dams
just upstream of Marsh Fork Elementary.

Buy out the landowners,
the stubborn ones will soon succumb
to fly rock and floods.

Raze Kayford, Zeb and Blair.

Strip Appalachia's coat of many colors.
Leave the mountain man lying
pitted and gray
unable to rise,
his head hollowed of dreams. ✤

What Stays

I remember Mom's washing machine loaded full
cleaning cucumbers while mason jars steamed,
glistened but I never helped her pack the pickles,
never learned her secret brine.

One Tuesday, my dog Peggy wouldn't
wake up. I shook and shook her. Still I had
to go to school that day. For a whole year
I imagined her outside my classroom window,
jumping hurdles, running through chutes
as if in a competition.

That spring biking home I drove into a parked
Pontiac because I didn't know how to turn.
As I picked up my bike walked it around the car
I saw the woman inside pretending not to notice me.

I remember the principal's office, his voice
like Dean Martin's, soothing, familiar,
but I don't remember why I was there.

Often I hear Dad at his clanking printing press, shifting
levers, black stained half moons under his nails.

Sometimes I feel Mom's magical
hands in my hair before church, shining up the blonde.

Back then in an abandoned dusky parking lot, Wanda,
Patsy and I, Charlie's Angels, brandished our weapons,

but then boys came down the hall
    between subjects, between poems, track meets,
  rating me a six

then the school dance I wasn't supposed to attend
and Brian Huck's spearmint cigarette kisses.

In our home with green velvet wallpaper,
my sisters and I pressed against the bathroom mirror, giving
boy advice as if we knew, as if none of us would break
    beneath a man.

And Aunt Jackie still gallops
through my head, still stares at my graduation photo and
asks, *how did the photographer make you so pretty?*

Other times, if I remember, if I close my eyes and think
    soft,
reach out my arms and feel a chestnut horse beneath me,
I hear that cowboy I almost loved, taking away my fear. ✽

Picture Day—Grade Two

We line up alphabetically.
I'm fourth.
The boy behind me practices his Shaun Cassidy smile.
The reedy photographer
flings an orange scarf over his shoulder,
clicks his black shoes across the gym floor.
He straightens and pats the beautiful ones
mutters French at the ordinary and the ugly.
I try not to chew my hair.
The girls from Elizabeth Avenue freshen their lip gloss.

In my favorite dress,
red, with Laurel and Hardy faces,
I pose, shoulders back, ankles crossed.
His great staccato eye peers through the lens

        then pauses…

And just like last year
he comes at me, licking his soft, bulbous thumb
to wipe the skin above my left eyebrow.
When my birthmark doesn't erase,
he sighs, returns, snaps.

Sometimes even now brushing my hair,
trying to be beautiful,
even though I've grown my eyebrows thick to hide it
even though the perfect redhead at the Sanskrit Spa
coos over my brows, blonde with soft brown streaks,
even still, I can feel his thumb. ✤

Escapes

In the cupboard of my mind
behind chapped lips and beneath chewed hair
apple trees twitch and an old aproned woman scolds.

When we were seven the garbage man thought
I was a boy
and you a girl.

Our teachers held us back.
You whispered fear
but I didn't care —
those so-immaculate ones!

My mother worried,
yours abandoned you
in her mind
doted on your brothers, made them caramel pudding
and sent you to bed.

The well-behaved logical kids moved on
loved and coveted.

You floated newspaper boats down gutters
after storms when we hid
in the orchard waiting
to glimpse the gnarled woman,
sneak a Golden Delicious from the basket on her porch,
hear her frail screech.

This morning I visit the church where we grew up
and there you are, handsome as belief,
rocking a tiny girl in your arms,
proud as God on the seventh day.

We smile at each other, bold, happy.

Once in the orchard
in an ancient Buick with one wheel
we planned our escape
from the words you couldn't pronounce,
from the math problems I never solved. ❋

Into Forever

Wool scarves blazing, figure eights and bunny hops,
Dad kneeling in the snow, tightening my laces,

long line of boys holding hands, skating round and round,
      fast as Christmas, a sudden snap of arms,
          flinging off the last one.

Trees holding ice, the sun out but not working,
the sun never works in January, in Ontario, in Elmira,
   on Earl's pond.

Fields of snow like little girls all glittered up,
grownups stirring hot cider, thick blankets from car trunks.

It was then you were flung off too, in a red truck in the
   woods,
                a thousand miles away. ❊

Forgiveness

Fixed up a bike from the junkyard
when I was ten.
Blue spray paint, knobby tires,
plastic leather seat, an imitation BMX.

But Saturday when I came out of the store
at The Old Mill it was gone.

Two days later I saw it leaning
against that house that used to be a bar.

Dad said we had to wait till Saturday.
The house looked like an overgrown garage
with busted windows.
The mailbox said "Burtlan" in shiny black letters.
Mr. Burtlan spoke with a cigarette hanging
out the left corner of his mouth.
He wore a thin white undershirt
that didn't cover his beer-belly.

There was my Dad
holding his Bible
saying we weren't going to call the police,
that they could keep the bike.
He said something about Jesus.
I felt rotten about wanting my bike back.

Mr. Burtlan said his boys found it in the field,
rode it on the ice, he thought they'd get hurt
so he slashed the tires.
Those tires cost me a whole month's allowance.

I thought of other passages
like a lying tongue is worse than...
sin no more, repent....
give me back my bike.
What about the time I ripped up my brother's Steve
    Carlton card.
I had to pick one of Dad's belts to get whipped.

Then Dad asked Mr. Burtlan about their stereo.
It was lying in pieces on the kitchen table.
There were Grateful Dead and Led Zeppelin tapes
    everywhere.
I wasn't allowed to listen to rock.
Dad offered them our stereo.
I knew Dad wouldn't buy another one,
he seemed a lot like Jesus
but I was embarrassed and wanted to get out of there.

Sometimes I don't know how to be Christ-like
were those boys listening behind a bedroom door,
did they think my Dad a push-over?
Was he showing off?
Was he a saint?
Did they get it?
Or did they just play Pink Floyd loud
on our stereo? ✽

What I Stole

was a Sunday School globe the size of a softball.
The oceans were cobalt blue, Canada, red,
Australia and New Zealand, purple.

Eileen told us we should tithe our allowance.
She pointed to Nigeria and said
the money would feed kids just like us
who liked to climb trees and play hide-and-seek,
only these kids hadn't enough to eat.
Greg asked if they didn't have grandmothers.

We filled the world with our nickels and dimes
at the beginning of class.
Later Eileen counted the coins,
slid them under the door with our attendance sheet.

While she read about Jesus
feeding the five thousand
I stared at the oceans and wondered
if they really did turn pale at the edges.

I kept thinking how good Peru, India and the Gold Coast
would look on my dresser.

After class, after everyone left
I slipped the world down my jumper.

But in my room the earth turned cold and tin.
I had to hide it from Mom.
I was too afraid to take it out and dream
of living in a green or yellow place.

The next Sunday
Eileen said the globe was missing
and she hoped whoever took it would bring it back,
that we needed it to feed the children.
I thought we could just put the money in an envelope.

I can't remember what I did with it,
too scared to bring it back,
probably threw it out.
Even now I reach for bright shiny things
to make me happy.
I have a whole drawer full
of honey luster and pink beach lipsticks,
a sample face the make-up artist at MAC drew
showing how to widen my eyes, contour my cheeks.
My closet is half filled with Guatemalan clothing,
multicolored serapes, fiesta skirts,
that look ridiculous on my white five foot ten boy figure.

Sometimes I think I can hear Eileen and Jesus
laughing behind the jackets, wondering if I'll ever learn. ✤

Grade Eight

I dream of Jason swinging his arm around my shoulders,
whispering something wonderful.
At thirteen he throws away his violin
and jingles girlfriends like loose change.

At recess my friends and I make fun of all the popular
girls with their highlighted hair and pierced ears.

In the hallway Jill and her new breasts
eclipse talk of football.
And flat chested Annie is still in the cool crowd
but slipping.

When Rob complains his balls itch and
wonders if one of us girls would like to scratch them
Cathy looks puzzled and asks, *You have more than one?*

At lunch I try to make my dreams come true
reciting the alphabet, twisting my apple stem,
forcing it to break at J,
the first letter of my true love's name.

Biking down Fifth Avenue, I wonder what life is like
inside those houses the size of banks
with bonsai trees shaped like geometry lessons
and white fenced backyards with turquoise pools.
Susan says she has no tan lines.

For grade eight graduation I stand far away from Susan
whose dress is exactly like mine
but she looks like Farrah Fawcett
and I some wanna-be.
I ask Bobby LaRue to dance,
he declines, he's some odd religion and isn't allowed.
I don't believe him. I gulp the gym air, squeeze my eyes shut
and in my mind cross myself like a Catholic would for luck.
I ask Jason, when he looks at me I feel like math homework.
Sure, he says, *let me finish my Coke.*
I sit, silently humming Stairway to Heaven,
the song almost gone when he nods. ✤

Saving Maynard

While the pastor drones on
I watch Maynard, his granite shoulders, disheveled hair.
I finger the dinosaur he carved on this pew
when he was six, his name in big awkward letters.
At sixteen he still comes because he has to,
to play church league hockey.
He sits beside his brother Darrell,
who, at dim basement parties with beer,
two-steps and tangos like a god,
a Mennonite dancing, a forbidden danger.

Maynard seldom speaks
hangs with tattooed people at places I only hear of.
Thursday nights at the arena among sharp sounds of skates
Maynard, padded and armored, a modern knight,
glides back and forth guarding his net
ready to fling sideways, kneel and slide.
His giant black gloves slap and suck the puck like a toy.

His mother watches him, worries
about more than this game.

One Friday night, bored or curious,
he joins us for youth group.

Afterwards in the dark church parking lot
the dilemma: whose place to crash.
Eleven o'clock; too late to go just anywhere.
Maynard suggests his house
but we protest: *What will your mom say?*
Maynard throws up his hands and in a woman's voice cries,
Hallelujah! the boy's been saved!

So fifteen bodies squeeze into cars
drive to a farm house surrounded by evergreens.
Downstairs Maynard plays Eric Clapton's "Cocaine";
above, in her nightgown, his mother beams,
makes lemonade, fills platters with soft cheese,
summer sausage
and slices of dark bread rich as redemption. ✽

The Mennonite Relief Sale

In a dusty flat Hispanic town
four girls and I, fresh from college, begin in a new home.
Like our grandmothers
we sun tea in the backyard and bake lentils,
knit blue cotton sweaters and mend work clothes.
But we know how to replace shingles,
change tires, question our bald-headed preacher.
We play pool and drink Coke Saturday nights at Abe's.
Summer evenings we roast chilies
listening to the Cowboy Junkies,
dreaming of Mennonite boys with rhythm.

We wonder if we'll stay with the church,
what we'll change, throw away, clutch.

Linda misses home, farm country,
straw hats and suspenders,
the thick sounds of Pennsylvania Dutch.
So we patch our favorite jeans with flannel hearts,
French braid our hair
and head off on a three-hour road trip
in the old Subaru, yelling quilt names:
Ohio Rose, Tumbling Blocks, Drunkard's Path.

Loud, beautiful and braless
we lift our tie-dyed T-shirts
to flash men in Jeeps and convertibles
like handing out blessings.

Two boys lip-synching to Meatloaf
follow us twenty miles.

In Rocky Ford
we find the fairgrounds.
Mennonites load tables with carrots and tomatoes,
bushels of cantaloupes, jars of warm apple butter.
We drink cider and eat sausage and kraut sandwiches,
listen to the auctioneer sell antique rocking horses,
handmade hope chests.
Outside the barn we find wrinkled, laughing women
slicing fresh strawberry pies.
They try to connect us to them,
figure out where we come from,
who our grandparents are.

I want them,
their thick useful hands,
their bantering like chickens
but I want my independence, too:
that woman hopping off her Silver Wing,
her long grey braid swaying from her helmet
saddle bags full of home preserves
wrapped in rag-weaved blankets. ❋

Easter Sunday

All dressed up for God, we crowd the church
our children well behaved with visions
of chocolate and bright colored eggs.
The pastor, suited up happy, begins.
When suddenly thirty-three year old Gary
leaps from his pew and proclaims
he is The Christ returned to us this day, Hallelujah.

He glows like a virgin before the bridegroom.
He forgives us, us, who called the police
after he attempted to pluck his right eye from its socket.
He smiles benevolently at his mother
as if pardoning her for signing the papers
for the psychiatric ward.

I wonder if all the Old Testament prophets
were just undiagnosed schizophrenics,
Moses seeing a burning bush,
Aaron with his staff turning into a snake,
Jonah living three days in a whale.
Think how we use these men to
haunt our children into obedience.

The children are ushered out
by Sunday school attendants
while elders in the front rows rumble discontent
and the stiff faced organist crescendos her hymn
against Babel.

What else can we in the back pews do
but walk Jesus home to his wife
and pray that God finds this, his lost son. �֍

What's in the Blood

they are not of the world
any more than I am of the world
— John 17:14

Great-Grandpa Daniel Horst
bought a model T-Ford truck
to transport vegetables to market.
Old Orders weren't allowed such things
but the bishop never said a word.

Not until the eldest son's wedding.
Just before the food
Daniel and his wife Annie
were excommunicated
and not allowed to sit at the first table.
Their three-year-old, Osiah,
remembers the buggy ride home.

We great-grandchildren
like to think that truck
was fire-engine red.

Still Annie kept dressing like an Old Order
all her life
in subdued cape dresses
hair in a bun
under a white starched covering,
collecting eggs in the hen house.
You can't excommunicate faith.

Their son Moses
forty-two in the family photo
wears a pin striped suit
a gold tie clip
a pocket watch
a smile
like a mobster
but he and all the children stayed Mennonite.

Their daughter Liddy Ann married a man
who would be chosen by lot
to become a preacher
who would yell the words of God
for thirty-nine years.

I like to think
there's a little bit of Daniel in me
buying a sheep farm
building a barn
dreaming of chickens
and a huge garden.
But oh how I wish I loved growing things
the hard work of planting more than enough
of sharing and canning for winter.
Next year, I vow, twenty rows of corn
while my husband buys a used
forty-dollar tiller
which he will spend hours fixing.
It's a good one, he says
grinning like an Old Order at auction.

Great Uncle Osiah was told by conference
to preach against wedding bands.
He thought it foolish
and obeyed for only a little.

I wear a plain band
no diamonds
just one emerald
left by Great Aunt Salinda,
a husband's wedding gift
no one saw her wear.

Osiah's bride wanted flowers
had them ordered
then cancelled.
Her father called them ostentatious
a word he never used before.

Three generations later
what would Bishop Ezra Martin say
at my wedding
as I carried white lilies
but refused a long fancy dress, a train, a veil.
Instead, a navy knee-length
which some worldly friend
said looked like a cape dress. ✻

Ways of Being

Let forgiveness pour in that open space
feel a new rhythm under feet.

Stop yelling at stray dogs.

Watch for the eternal.
See the meadow unfold a dancing girl
in pink chiffon and mittens.

Listen to the sky murmuring.

Bear witness.
Carry warm cups of cider on a tray
down a busy street.

When teenagers call
invite them to come right away,
let the laundry wait, don't mop the floor
instead prepare love.

If that raku mug breaks,
    let it go.

Imagine a lover washing your hair.

Feel the muddy spots of earth
the rough hands of a neighbor
bring him warm rye bread and wine.

Go feed the sheep like a prayer.

Can you think of someone alone?
Be to them a thick wool blanket.

If no one does anything kind for you
perhaps they have none to spare.

Find a quiet way to sit, soften your eyes
drift away, come gentle.

Lick the fingers of God
He has been stirring love forever. ❁

Light Waking

(for Darlene)

through my window a remembered dancing
you and I in thick cotton nightgowns
turning wild sweet rhythms in the sun

sisters in the same room
leaping from bed to bed
over a river full of alligators

on the living room carpet
Dad sprawled in a patch of sun
a horse, a king, a floor

by Queen Anne's lace
in the field spinning mice
your hand grasps mine

husbands take us away
we bring our Grandmother's quilts

you cross a whole country
I look after your home, your children,
every night your boy checks the riverbank
a mother turtle, back legs spraying sand
nesting eggs

tonight I lie in your bed
and imagine you touring wineries with the wives
I leaf through your books
your children downstairs
quiet
I wait for the waking
morning hockey in the drive

when you come back we will dance
curtains open
let the neighbors walk by
you and I unraveling in the sun ✤

Beliefs

I used to believe in my babysitter,
Big Red Gum, Breck hair
bell-bottoms and boyfriends,

that the Bee Gees could save a soul from sadness,

that God was between black leather covers
his voice like Grandpa's, booming and bass,
arms raised in ecstasy,

that the neighbor boy with permed hair and farm hands
would someday love me
and we would run cattle in Saskatchewan,

that everyone should be Mennonite,
eat homemade whoopie pies and protest war.

Now I believe in the junkyard man who can't read
but owns half this town,
his daughter who hangs ham in the shed for months
and cuts off the mold just before dinner,

in Mrs. Frey, my white wooly ewe
who lets all the lambs climb and jump off her back,

in my Mother's voice every other Sunday night
long distance, wanting me home,

in my dog's morning moans,
in yoga and poets,
that redhead from Belington
who says good is not always nice.

I believe in beauty,
the three Hooded Warblers
lined up on my windowsill, peering in. ❧

Resurrection

When it starts I run to the red oak, watch and pray;
at dawn the macarena rumbles through the woods
and I dance a benediction
before being chased wildly home, rolled over in the leaves.

This crazy God thing is everywhere.

It is the warmth of a bald woman, lying in bed
pink-hatted, unable to move,

the flying red cape of the neighbor boy,
sword drawn, chasing the invisible down the drive.

It is hunger on the first day of winter
I eat and eat and never am full.

It is my grandfather saying goodbye, holding Grandma's
    hand
        while we sing "How Great Thou Art,"
           squinting at the brightness
             and smiling. ✿

Beginnings

We were hoping for a man,
an end to this nunnery,
thrilled you were finally coming
but we had a party beforehand
just in case you were the kind
who sings hymns Friday nights.

You came when the kitchen and backyard
were filled with the smell of roasting chilies.
It made you nauseous
so you went out front for fresh air,
weeded the flowerbed
pulled the columbines with the thistles.

Your room was across the hall from mine;
we hardly spoke for weeks.

The first time we hiked alone
I dressed in cut-offs and white socks
pulled up to my knees.
You said only middle aged men with plaid shorts
wore their socks that way.

One Saturday night
you did thirty pull ups
on the bar between the kitchen and laundry room,
took a twenty-minute shower,
then left to take two girls to some movie.
I had to date the dentist
and listen to details of impacted molars
and crying children.
He talked like a chihuahua
and smelled of Milk-Bones.

Braless in a thin blue cotton shirt
I helped you change
the muffler on the Omni.
You weren't afraid of anything.
You opened lawn mowers and roofs to fix,
got old Mrs. Byler to tell wild stories
no one else knew she had.
You drove an orange Scout,
found work for homeless men,
and you were gorgeous.

At the Thanksgiving celebration
I caught you watching me.
That evening we walked for miles
talking about work, our shattered images of God,
how rich and silent Mennonites were becoming,
how only the Catholic Church seemed to know
the evils of the Gulf War.
Laughing Hispanic women were patting tortillas
into perfect circles outside their trailers.

I was so sure you'd kiss me
when we tobogganed in the San Juan Mountains.
And Christmas Eve after midnight mass
we never even held hands.

It felt like years
until you touched me by the Conejos river
by the white lights of Our Lady of Guadalupe.

This morning you nibble my bare shoulders
make huevos rancheros,
serve orange juice in wine glasses.

It seems when I was little
I reached over to the pillow beside me
expecting you to be there. ❧

Aunt Margaret's Wedding Gift

Aunt Margaret laughs and asks if my fiancé is poor.
My left hand flung out towards her
showing off my homemade engagement ring.

In the kitchen my sister wraps pieces of iced fruitcake
    in lace
for the reception, for little girls to put under their pillows
and dream of husbands.
In the basement Grandpa and my fiancé work at the
    scroll saw,
where they cut an oak frame heart for the wedding cake.

Outside the soon-to-be best man from San Antonio
throws his head back and spins
catching snowflakes on his tongue.
Margaret wonders aloud if his lane doesn't meet the road.

Mom calls everyone to the living room for refreshments.
Aunt Margaret and Uncle Jack hand me a
    red-ribboned box.
It's a soup tureen, ivory with day lilies painted all around,
ideal for a family of nine or a woman who throws
    lavish parties.
Before I can say thank you,
My aunt opens her poinsettia lips:
That pattern you chose certainly was expensive.
You picked that with your last boyfriend, Tom, right?
that handsome Russian Mennonite your mom so hoped
    you'd marry.

That tureen is very heavy so do be careful, dear, but if it breaks
  it breaks.
She piles five strawberry-shaped cookies in her hand
from a silver tray and plunges herself back into the couch.
My uncle studies his shoes.
My fiancé winks at me and refills everyone's coffee,
entertained by the awkwardness of the afternoon.

Years later he will smile and announce to our guests,
We'll be serving cream of asparagus tonight
out of Tom's tureen, so do be careful. It's very heavy
  and expensive;
but then again, if it breaks it breaks. ✤

On Trying to Name One Good Kiss

the one I waited for, forever,
the fairytale, Christmas Eve in the sand

or possibly the one at Bear Haven
when we laid down in the pines

maybe the one in Wal-Mart after I turned thirty-five
and, crying, demanded a decision, my eggs numbered

perhaps the one when he came back from Nicaragua
after telling stories fast as a four-year-old
how he built a house on stilts and ate sea turtles

no, the one he placed in my hair while I lay
propped with pillows in a hospital bed,
red-eyed machines blinking like harlots, and us
not knowing yet what had been taken. ❧

Afternoon Writing

I sharpen three pencils,
gather blue and purple pens

but the laundry basket hisses
under its mound of angry cotton

I steep peppermint tea with honey
read a George Ella poem to warm up

but the glasses on the countertop
spew their milky films at her stanzas

and the dog hair on the pine floor
spins a slow waltz with the breeze
gathering partners like a rich playboy

I put down a few words
ornamental, incantation, goldfinch feathers

but the soap scummed shower
is clanging its metal plug

and the stovetop reaches its oily fingers
into my head

my notebook waits
the stripping of nice things
the dangerous words

No! the bleach bottle is yelling
and Grandma's ghost in the spare room by the boxes
        and dust
is shaking her head, *oh dear, oh dear*

the spiders lace their amusements in the corner
the rugs fade into footprints
the curtains exhale their old-man breath

don't tell
what you think
        where you hide
who you are

the dining room is shouting like a border guard
spray Windex, pour Murphy's Oil
your house like your head is a mess
clean up what the neighbors can see ✤

Work Site

Could you come a little closer Chief
with your clipboard and your hardhat?
Could you lean over from your other projects
and point a work-stained finger down
and say, *You girl, you and I?*

Could you aim your fat belly sun over my little patch
of life for just a few days?

Could you let me know what stuff
in that black book of yours is real
and what is just for bragging rights and chaos?

Could you show me the way back to the garden,
teach me how to harvest asparagus?

This autumn could you stripe my maple leaves
pink and blue so I would know for sure
all those generations didn't
make you up Chief?

If I say, *Now on the count of three
blow this flower from my hand*——

Oh Chief I'm so weary from working
with no direction, no site supervision.
How about sending down some blueprints?
I'm tired of guessing on the electric. ✿

What I Don't Want to See

a girl's buttocks cupped in pink panties
overflowing her low-rise jeans

shiny Japanese beetles mating on the porch

men in white summer pants
useless as cream filling
who can't fix a dripping faucet

eight days of rain and no hay put up

the neighbor picking watermelons in the dark
muttering about his wife

two spiders by the printer
their spent pile of round black bugs

the crisp-linened woman
who smells like the spring issue of *Vogue*
who looks past me when I speak

the hairy-eared song leader patting a sixteen-year-old rump
in three-quarter time

a thin gray mouse snapped dead
in a plastic trap with cheese

Frankie with his pool cue, unbuttoned shirt,
a golden Jesus crucified in a thicket of dark hair ❀

Bodies... The Exhibition

Saturday six p.m. silver haired couples in savvy shoes,
city boys sporting high bosomed girls,
parents with children polite as gingerbread,
stand in line, as if waiting to see a Broadway musical.

In a church-like hush
we wander windowless rooms full of cadavers,
peeled, probed, plasticized.
Four play cards, one drop kicks a soccer ball.

A human's clean, white scapula
lies next to a whale's,
suggests evolution,
this the only bone that floats free of the skeleton.

A glittery girl glances over tables of
phalanges, a pharynx, an esophagus.
Her sighing mother instructs, *Slow down,
read, learn something.*

In the little green pamphlet
put out by the Catholics
we are urged to remember
these bodies belonged to real people
who may benefit from our prayers
for the repose of their souls.
I imagine spirits trapped against the black ceiling
watching us watch them.

Signs say don't touch
but without guards or glass
a young woman in floral fingers a spleen.

A man's skin lies flat and lonely
like a discarded winter coat, outgrown,
the hood prickling with new hair.
My husband skins deer
hangs them in the barn from a huge metal hook.
Most people don't look long.

A man who smells of cats
pats his horror-stricken wife and says
they're not real people.

Staring at a glass-boxed neon heart
a woman explains to her teenage son
where his hole was
how the surgeon patched it
how she prayed.

An aortic artery hangs like a rope
this is what broke in Uncle Rich
March 10th in the afternoon.

Two three-lobed lungs lie side by side
one pink, one truly black just as Mr. Reed said
in grade eight health.
Above, white wavy letters
one pack of cigarettes can shorten your life
by three and a half hours.
An offering box big as a school boy
stands three-quarters full
of Salems, Marlboros, a few Winston Lights.

The only room with a warning
holds little lighted bones in glass cylinders
perfect unborn fingers, knees, toes.
At the row's end a full term wrinkled girl frozen
in a C-curve
a mass of nerves protruding from her spine like a fist.

A female's disconnected pelvis tilts upwards
the gray gelatinous labia open.
Above, a tiny white label proclaims the clitoris
that coveted pink bead.
Two prepubescent boys giggle
quickly walk away, and return.

In the final room I hold a human heart, a brain,
stare mesmerized at the woman erect in the corner
half-peeled like an orange.

Afterwards we eat Italian
and I can't help but watch
the chestnut-haired girl at the table next to us
in her backless dress,
her exposed scapula, misshapen,
birth defect or some terrible accident.

In the bathroom
I can't stop picturing my insides,
the vessels like roadmaps of chaotic cities,
the mechanical advantage of muscle to bone,
tenderloin, rump roast.

Back in the hotel I can't imagine making love.
Unable to sleep we rise early,
work out in the gym on stationary bikes
visualizing our hamstrings and quadriceps
contracting, relaxing without us. ✽

Wanting to Sing Hymns

Sometimes, when I'm alone, I start the day practicing
do, re, mi, fa, sol, la, ti, do
as if I'm an authentic Mennonite
getting ready for a day of work and gratitude.
My notes teeter and fall
but it's my Dad's voice I imagine filling the loft,
his long throat, full chest.

I remember hearing him on a city stage when I was nine,
elegant men singing Haydn's *Creation*,
tenors innocent as dawn,
the omnipotent bass,
God swinging his feet in the rafters
keeping time.

That year Dad signed me up
for the Mennonite Children's Choir.
All those good kids, bunches of them standing on the stage.
I knew only Cathy.
She was saintly and didn't know the anatomy of boys,
just music, shape notes, crescendos, fermatas,
quarter rests, half rests.
I couldn't keep up, stand still, read a D from an E.
The director knew lip-synching when he saw it.
One Tuesday night, my stomach heavy as a puck,
my head in an earthquake, I crept out, hid in the hall.
Mom understood. Dad didn't say a thing.

For my sister's wedding he sang *Sunrise, Sunset.*
His warmth washing over us.
Even Aunt Margaret cried.

Every long distance call he tells me about his latest concert,
his last solo, the acoustics of high stone Catholic churches.

I sing loud with the Glad Tidings Quartet on my stereo
or quietly Sunday in the pew. Never in a choir
or on a porch. Never as a gift.

Still I practice scales
when the house is empty
open the red hymnal,
harmonize with the perking coffee, the popping toast,
the boiling oatmeal. ✤

Patches called Philippi

Stretching against the courthouse gazebo
Mr. Zickefoose readies himself to run through town waking
against the foothills of the Allegheny,
notes of hymns tumbling from College Hill.

Jake, eighty-two with a loose face, large smile,
three silver keys hanging from his belt
walks four miles every day but Sunday,
his wooden cane like an exclamation mark
pointing at dogwood trees, their waxy white blooms.

Fourth generation Philippians color their lawns
an obligated beauty
purple creeping phlox, bearded irises, snowdrops.

Small morning crowds gather in the City Restaurant
biscuits and gravy
catching up
who's at the funeral home, the heavy rain last night
how at the fair's livestock auction Senator Minear
bought eleven-year-old Cody's lamb
for sixteen hundred and ten dollars
the value of a whole flock.

In the fall men settle into the deep woods
hollow knocking of a woodpecker
a bucked-up sapling
a raccoon returning to its den tree for the day
the quiet of hunters lingers
through thermoses of coffee and pockets of candy bars.

In winter rhododendron leaves curl against cold,
    exotic cigars.

All year the rhythmic rocking of the CSX down the grade
    hauls coal,
ninety-some cars with Chessie Cats
and graffiti painted in New York or Oklahoma.

This town full of history, rich black as diamonds.

In 1852 Lemuel horsebacked to Richmond
his model covered bridge in his saddlebag.
Using two chairs as abutments, he stood on it.
Philippi's famous bridge, mortise, tenons, trunnels
that bad weather and typhoid couldn't halt
which a toll helped pay for,
five cents for an empty cart,
ten cents for a score of hogs,
twenty cents for a Jersey wagon without springs.

Strong as the people this bridge
Civil War bullets in its yellow poplar.
Rev. Joshua knelt three hours in prayer for its survival.
An officer, ordered to burn the bridge, throwing his torch in
    the river.
That prayer still lingers, saving it from floods, ice jams,
    a fire.

After the '85 flood, the town's mummies reclined
as if sunning themselves
for three afternoons on Bigfoot Byrer's front lawn.
Now in an old bathroom in the abandoned railroad depot
you can see them, for one dollar hear the stories
from a flower-hatted lady
how a local farmer got two cadavers
from the mental hospital
claimed the Bible taught him to embalm
how they toured Europe with P. T. Barnum's circus.

In the nineties Veda walked the streets
in snake-skinned pants
and silver sequins.
She cast spells
and had remedies to cure warts and baldness,
stole tomatoes from Mrs. Cole's garden
and gave them as gifts.

For a hundred years a stained-glass Jesus has held his lamb
and soothed the night on Walnut Street.

Saturday afternoons teenaged boys
with loud jokes and cigarettes
fish bass from a johnboat
always polite enough to ask how you are, what's new.
    Sometimes midnight lovers
stand on the walkway of the bridge and watch deer crossing
against the north flow of the Tygart.

Churches stand crisp white and steepled
tightly held in hollers and on hillsides
welcome signs
hymns flung out Sunday mornings.

The gray-haired would-be cowboy
swaggers to town two, three times a week
wearing a tin badge and holster, its six-shooter confiscated.
He goes to Moe's or Bernie's pool hall where they feed him
    for free
and drive him home when it's rainy or cold.

This town where the least are looked after,
where people believe in life, gardens and graduation
the spring full of children sharing bikes,
parents and innocence
where home spills onto the sidewalks and drifts to the edge
    of the woods. ❁

Grantsville Stockyards

Dennis struts in chewing straw
and I follow immersed in the manure-laden air.
We sit on a stiff bench
next to two clean-faced Amish boys
with ruddy cheeks.

They understand the buyers
old and limping
muscular and beer-bellied
with ball caps advertising feed mills.
These boys have ridden pigs,
thrown fresh eggs at younger brothers,
helped birth calves,
held downy chicks against their cheeks.
Fifteen, already knowing their world
how to breed and slaughter,
to comfort themselves with food.

The auctioneer, clean-shaven
in a crisp white shirt
begins
his voice like river water over stones
sells dry cottage cheese, homemade yogurt,
radishes and ramps.

When raisin pies with crimp crusts come
the camouflaged man behind me buys three
rubbing his belly like a well-earned prize.

Packages of puffed cheese curls come next,
kids squeal, tug at their Dad's plaid sleeves,
old men resurrect from sleep, wink their bids
the auctioneer's voice crescendos,
a preacher selling happiness.

Then Holstein calves *by the head, four to go*
a black horse *two years old, two months bred*
men in worn-out jeans grunt, prod, spit.

A woman beside me reads *Guideposts*
while her husband in loose bib overalls
chuckles at the men who pay too much
for cows or goats.

I'm glad I'm not a hog
obese and naked,
shocked and kicked,
my weight advertised in bright yellow bulbs.

I wish I were like the brunette down front
holstered pliers at her hip
comfortable in her hard beauty,
correcting the auctioneer when he loses the bid.

Big brown eggs sell in batches of eight to ten dozen
for angel food cakes women will sell from their kitchens.

An awkward-grinning man, fly gapped open,
shirt buttons bulging against his greasy belly,
lifts bantam roosters, peacocks,
passes them down the rows by their feet.
A Rhode Island Red pecks free
flaps over the gasping crowd
toward the rafters, toward freedom,
before getting plucked down by a spry well-wrinkled
    woman.

In the pickup on the way home
the goat cheese reminds me of barn boots
and the thick slabs of home-churned butter
just look too white.
I shudder at the thought of some day getting chickens
of collecting the shit-covered eggs.
And I wonder if I'll ever be a farmer
as I pretend I am to my friends. ✤

The Dirt Road

That old man was nothing but good.
When he come the first night to stay with Mama and me
he brought pepperoni rolls and milk.
I called him Dad, me forty-two.

Last Tuesday he sent me for snuff
even though my truck was part run down.
When I come back I yell but don't find him
then there he is in that rotting shed, rope round his neck
legs still swinging.
It's a wonder that rafter held.

When Mama died he went crazy,
up all night, sleep all day
never once thought about our neighbor
needing help with the cows.
So I done his share too
drove posts, stapled wire.
Man could break his back throwing that maul in the heat.
Cows got out twice before I was done
spent half one night looking for 'em.
They'd went all the way to Hackers Creek,
looking slow and stupid but they ain't.

I'll borry Dad's green flannel shirt
and cowboy boots for the funeral, his Aqua Velva.
Left half a blue bottle in the bathroom.
He won't mind.

I don't remember my first dad
he was killed on Rt. 92
drove into a telephone pole
laid in the truck passed out.
It was Feb. and he was froze when they found him.

I been studying on something.
That story of Lazarus, how he got raised back up.
His family didn't have to wait for no heaven to see him
     again.
Martha had Mary to help pester Jesus;
me I ain't got no one no more.
Musta been nice to have them sisters looking after you,
Jesus walking down your dirt road. ❧

Laughing Jenny and the Cowboy

Is her husband dead yet? we wonder
as Jenny leaves Bernie's Pool Hall giggling,
the cowboy brushing back her wild curls.
Sipping steamed eggnog we gaze at them
through the coffee shop window.
In the snowy night he struts,
a toy sheriff's badge on his puffed out chest,
a tin pistol on his holster.
Everyone knows Mr. Norris bought that new ten-gallon
    black hat,
had it set out at the thrift store just before the cowboy's
    ritual visit.
Jenny caresses a fake fur coat over her belly,
swollen with a tumor or something unborn.

We know her husband got shipped to Quiet Hills
after sitting two years in a lopsided recliner
yelling every time he hurt or got confused
and pulled out his catheter.
Twenty-four years older than she,
his prize, she who slept alone in the back
behind a faded flowered sheet.
Now her niece has put her in a flimsy trailer
    on Dog Town Road
and is good at explaining, so the checks keep coming
and the food stamps.
Jenny uses the cook stove for heat,
an old radio wheezes out country,
she dances with Hank Williams.

When Human Services shows up,
she makes coffee and jokes,
tells them her niece looks after her,
puts ointment on her sugar sores, sets out her medicines.
She knows hell would come if she told the truth.

Through the falling snow the cowboy's voice
makes thick white clouds,
his arms conducting some outrageous tale.
Jenny's face shines, proud and embarrassed.

We celebrate our fourteenth anniversary
quietly eating three-milk cake
and watch mesmerized through the window
slightly jealous. ✿

A Hard Cold Morning

The Ewe

We're in bed
when the front door opens
and Dennis yells
I need help in the field.
Call the vet.
Big Joanna
the one who sniffs us
and once slid her leg
in Dennis's coveralls trying to
get at the feed bucket—
is lying down in the field
her uterus out in the snow
a fresh black lamb standing at her side.

We heave her inside the barn
elevate her rump
over an old copper kettle.
Wash the red raw mass of suction cups.

Her uterus—if that's all it is—
is not like mine
mine: smooth, defined
unused, inside.

The vet made it sound gentle
an easy slide.
Mike holds her head,
my foamy hands open and push
but she isn't dilated
there's too much, my hands too big.
We decide it'll get twisted
we can't get it all back in
she'll get infected, suffer.

We let the little lamb nurse
while Dennis gets his gun.
He hates killing things.
I don't know where to stand
holding the lamb inside my jacket
telling him it's a hard, cold world
wiping off what afterbirth is left.

Seconds after the shot
we hear the ewe
kick against the pen.

Before Mike and Dennis haul the carcass
to the woods
we try to get the lamb to nurse
one more time
for the colostrum.
He won't.

In the far corner of the barn
we find his twin
so still
in its sac.

The Lamb

We name him Sammy
short for Samson or Sammy Sosa
a strong sturdy name.
He can't stand right
and falls down
won't drink much from the bottle.
In the house I wrap him
in an old flannel shirt,
arrange him in a metal washtub with hay
by the window
let him listen to Adventures in Good Music
while I'm at work.

But Thursday when I come home
his scent is gone
the washtub empty and clean.
Mike or Dennis must have found him dead.
I vacuum, put things away
gather up the Christmas cards
the nativity scene
after all it's almost the end of January.

The Afterdeath

The women at work
the carnivores wearing lipstick
who attend church like clockwork
they think I'm cruel, living on a farm
raising sheep
taking them to market.
They say they couldn't do it
imply how sweet and decent they are
living in town.
Come Monday they'll ask how Sammy is. ✤

In Sago

The preacher said, Jack Weaver scrawled *Jesus Saves*
in the coal dust, on the side of the mantrip
before they rode down into the mountain
the part God made black.
He said some of them men never left West Virginia,
that Junior Hamner grew up raising beef
just above where he died.
He said those men worked as brothers
doing what needed done,
their sweat holy,
if coal fails the country fails.

That crew was tough,
two miles in when hell exploded,
lightning struck, the fire damp lit.
Belt man died right then.

Smoke and gas rolled down the shaft
acrid dust settled on tongues.
They heaved timbers, hung brattice cloth on spads,
cocooned in a cross-cut.

An old miner in my Bible study
said they could have just walked out
the same way they came,
following the rails
down 2 Left and back Main
but they were taught *barricade in*.
They knew that oxygen in their rescuers
was good for one maybe two hours.
Lying side by side
in the cool damp black
the startling silence, broken by
popping coal ribs.

Ten maybe twelve hours passed,
talk of Jesus and cards drifted.
Not knowing if some were dead already,
Toler found an insurance application in his pocket,
wrote loose and jagged,
a blackened apparition saying
it isn't bad, it's just like sleep,
Tell All—I see Them on the other side,
I love you.

Who'd they see?
Aunt Maydell serving buttermilk and cornbread
wild John taking his with honey?
What were they thinking on? NASCAR and horseshoes,
a daughter in a red jacket
now photographed on the front of *USA Today*
crying by the tipple.

When Jesus died the earth cracked and trembled right then,
not before, rocks split, the sky darkened
and they barricaded him inside the mountain too
but he got free, walked outside,
as we prayed you would,
thirteen cap lamps bobbing out
piercing our darkness
with an unbelievable story. ❄

The House

an alarm clock turned off
quilts thinning on the bed
the dog stares out the window,
barks at nothing

the fern drops brown leaves on the floor
unopened mail strewn on the oak table
brown wool socks grow holes
the shoes have been empty for days
coats hang limp in the closet

the TV intrudes on cue

the milk and cereal tire of being poured
the coffee pot forsaken
the lid open and broken
like a life ✤

Intrusion

You come too close,
talk and talk and talk,
brazen and omnipotent,
stopping me from clearing brush from the fence.
You tell me how to use the machete,
what to plant next to the drive.
It begins to rain, you seem not to notice.
I try to interrupt,
tell you what I need, what I want,
it is small but you dismiss me.
The turquoise of my jacket bleeds down my thighs.
I want to walk away backwards without eyes, without feet,
from your logic, your permanence.
But you stand immaculate
(even in the rain)
success dripping from your hips.

Yesterday you joked with my friends
said poetry and farming are useless
as you lounged in my living room, devouring my food.
My husband claimed you didn't say that at all.
He sounded so right; I am tired of him too.

This morning I wake early
pour cold water over my head,
drive an hour from home,
to this cinnamon scented coffee shop.
I open my thick notebook and begin to write
but your hard marble eyes peer over my shoulder,
laughing.
I shift in the worn leather chair,
watch a man in green on his cell phone,
a couples' bitter eyes,
a girl who smells of cotton,
while you saunter my pasture of new lambs. ✽

Trying to Stay

In a blue glow the anchorman,
the worrying morning news.

I marvel that I am still here
in this pale body,
drinking creamed coffee
rearranging chores
until nothing gets done.

Out the window the limber laughing neighbors
plant asparagus and cauliflower.
Closing the blind, I ask
and my husband says, *Yes,*
you used to be more fun.

At the clinic in my nurse's uniform
feeling dumb as pajamas
I make little adjustments to the ill
draw up hope in sterile needles
my hands shaking over the sink.

I walk with my dog through the woods,
tell him my insufficiencies.
Once home, I scold myself for not noticing
if the tiny rubbery flowers became mushrooms,
if the wild blueberries were ripe.

To take away my sadness
I swallow a small white pill
as the thin young doctor instructed.
Before bed I work a Sudoku.

Saturday my husband and I go to the movies.
I watch the smooth-haired, the strutting
women who match shoes to scarves
enticing lovers with stunning precision.

In the whispering dark we hush
mesmerized by Beowulf,
by flying swords, choreographed slaughter.
From a watery cave, Grendel's Mother rises
wearing nothing but melted gold over her breasts,
        seducing the king
                for centuries.

Driving home I picture her slithering in,
pressing against my husband,
ordering me to the back seat.

Later she lounges on the chair by our bed
rates my performance with a small tsk, tsk.

Just before sleep
I imagine again
the escarpment on Rt. 78
the absence of guard rails
the bouncing and thrusting
the small stain. ❁

Another Day

As a girl Susan cut flowers out of crepe paper,
painted orange irises on barns,
stitched Sweet Williams on couch cushions.
She dreamed in begonias, wanted to make some small city
beautiful. Own a shop that gave free jasmine ice tea
to anyone.

Then Dave kissed her in the cornfield
one pure clean touch like dew.

Now tubes of acrylics crack in the closet
while she bathes and feeds five children
tucks her husband into every day
with a sack lunch of cold sausage and mustard,
two butterscotch squares.

Cleaning the cupboards,
Susan drifts to daydreams dangerous as dragons.
Desire sits on the sill and will not shoo.

She knows the devil, a snake with breasts who thinks too
    much.

She ponders the breaking down of dirt,
the roots of weeds, the afternoon storm.

As the rain stops
she lies down in the grass, next to worms
and expects robins to come.
Under the shifting shapes of clouds she waits
but there is no red-breasted epiphany.

Back inside she does the dishes,
folds laundry, answers math questions
as women often will. ❦

Mother from Paradise

Listen here, women.
In the beginning, every day
honeysuckled air, sprouting snow peas,
blooming orchids,
Adam yelling out names.
The serpent handsome as a ram
big horned and strutting.
God's voice an orchestra.

And then I plucked and bit that apple.
Adam ate too, he did anything I did back then.
God knew damn well we'd fall.
Afterwards, what a show
burning thunder, funereal wailing.
We saw our nakedness
my right breast smaller than my left
and that ugly bristle brush triangle,
Adam's hairy buttocks.
We were supposed to be the pinnacle.

God threw us baggy clothes and said, *Get out.*

My belly swelled like a pumpkin.
I squatted behind the beans screaming,
while Adam got all big eyed and clumsy.

Our first boy killed the second
over a gift God didn't like.

After that we stayed in the backyard
growing tomatoes, hot peppers and children.
New cities cheated farmers, fashioned orgies.
God threw a flood, picked out one family to save,
not like us, favor-less and farming.
Adam just kept on hoeing
repeating the same old repentance.
I left him.

Oh it goes on and on
burning sulfur, golden calves.
You know the rest.

Except the parts God allowed men to skew
like making Mary Magdalene a prostitute,
twisting Paul's words
to make us women silent slaves,
changing the Holy Spirit from a She to a He.

I couldn't leave you
with those bullies throwing that apple.

I am your Mother.
I stayed to midwife all your babies.
It's not your fault your Father cursed childbirth.

You are as brilliant as the garden,
as perceptive as the roots of spring,
creator of life.

Stop listening to God's stubble-faced cronies,
who love to hate us,
who thrust that apple between our lips
to shut us up.

Spit or swallow
but speak, dear daughter, speak. ✽

Shearing

Sarah thrashes like she's demon possessed
as Mike grabs, holds, flips
until she leans limp against his thighs
quits her sopranoed baas.

You would think she'd want
to get that dense dirty coat shorn.

Beads of sweat from Mike's brow drop into her wool.
Dennis, in last years blood-stained overalls, instructs,
open the belly wool first
good
go down
careful
watch her woowoo.

Professionals do one every five minutes,
a hundred and fifty per day at two dollars a head.

We shear five in two and a half hours,
tell stories in-between changing cutters
or sweeping excrement
while Brown-Eyed Susans sway in the field.

Saturday night at Wal-Mart on the clearance rack
a bright blue box glimmers at me.
Be Sensual. Go bare as the day you were born.
Brazilian wax.
$4.99

The next morning after church, dreaming of sex,
I heat the jar of honey gold, lock the bathroom.

The first pass feels like Dante's Inferno.
There's no way that hundred-and-ten pound
yellow-bikinied girl on the box ever did this to herself.
I think of the ewes, Esmeralda lying flaccid and panting,
the hot sun, the buzzing, the slips of the blade.

Afterwards I call my sister to whine about the pain.
She says she gave wax up years ago,
suggests boy-cut bikini bottoms.
She doesn't understand
it's not about looking good at the beach.

But Oh the sex was like Eden,
like that song of Madonna's, about the virgin.
A new thing to crave.

The next day in the barn
Sarah stands by the feed trough
stomps her right forefoot, snorts.
You would think she'd understand
she's done. It's the wooly ones we want.
From the pasture with the pond
Rambo watches, struts, practices his sensuality.
While the electric shears vibrate
I hold Esther's spotted face in my hands,
stare into her marble eyes,
There, There, I whisper,
think how the wind will cool your skin
and the sex is coming. Next Wednesday we'll let Rambo in. ✤

Spirit Friends

we are the glimmer of sunlight
tufts of white wool blowing from the fence

cool spring water from Middle Mountain

we are moss under bare feet
the red scents of summer

cotton shirts billowing on clotheslines

we are escaping
coming back, going there

we are needless, wantless and dancing

yet we are insatiable

we are an invitation
to an everlasting party

See the oaks?
we have grown her leaves big as hands

we are pockets of light caught by children

the healing of salve

we are the smell of bacon and eggs
black coffee in a waitress' full pot

we are the yearning of kisses

Come, be loved ❖

Heaven and Earth

The rain just started
and the mountains have disappeared
like the world stops at old route 250
and God and the afterlife
are in the thick cool mist
just beyond our neighbor's farmhouse,
his Suffolk sheep bleating their way to the barn.

Noisy in the kitchen
Mike mixes five pounds flour
three-quarter cup baking powder
enough pancake mix to last a month or two.
Pale gold maple syrup, a first run,
warms on the stove
as the smell of coffee drifts.

Soon he will kiss me, leave for work
and I'll stay hoping to get something done.

Esau barks to go out.
We get soaked fur and skin
chase and watch birds
the ones we haven't learned to name.

Then inside the crazy drying
rubbing with old towels,
lying on the living room rug, braided,
I imagine by a crinkly-skinned woman
filled with rag wisdom.

The rain rumbles deep and bass
like hunger
like all the things
I forget to feel on ordinary days.

Watching raindrops wiggle down the window
nothing needs to get done.

I belong here under this noise
the child of someone colorful and rhythmic
who makes the earth deepen
and the flowers and dirt loosen their scents. ✤

Yearnings

Mabel taught us we shouldn't want much.
Eight girls in Sunday School
crowded around a kidney shaped table.
She softly urged us to keep our desires simple and pure
so not to create greed, lust, vanity.
And there was Jesus on the flannel board
same robe and sandals every week,
same uncut hair and dusty feet,
eating nothing but white bread and fish.

In a tiny pale green room far from the world
Mabel gathered each of us in her garden-worn hands.
Her voice trembled the telling of a girl's request
for the head of John the Baptist on a silver platter.
The cushion of her belly held us safe
as she told of Jonah swallowed by a whale.
She scattered cranberry,
garbanzo and brown speckled cow beans.
Giggling, we sorted and glued
making peace doves and pebbled crosses as Mabel beamed.
When the buzzer sounded, her good-bye wave
gently threw us into a new week
of bullies and playgrounds.

Saturdays we girls biked to Shannon's early
to watch the *Flintstones*,
I Dream of Jeannie and *Bewitched*,
with cosmic commercials
for Pop Tarts, Ken dolls
and a Barbie Makeup Head on a pink platter
that we all wanted and begged for.
We brushed its eyelids blue, lips electric pink,
twirled and braided its shiny blonde hair
twenty-six different ways
before turning fourteen, wearing bikinis on Sauble Beach,
before leaving for college, some wandering across Canada,
one watching a husband die.

I wonder where you all are now,
if you lost Mabel too,
those prudent stories.

At forty the things I want now
multiply like Pharaoh's plagues.
I want shoes that tie up 'round my calves
dinner at restaurants this town doesn't have,
a drawer full of Victoria's Secrets
to curve my prairie chest and straight hips.

That raw red scar down my belly needs to vanish.
I want my eleven-year-old hair back, glossy and blonde,
that impudent smile from grade two
the belief that everyone loves me.

I want to get famous
write poetry like anne sexton
read a fan letter before bed.

Now, standing in front of the bedroom mirror
deciding if my Miracle Bra is performing,
I think of Mabel, beautiful in a flowered dress
laughter wrinkling face,
how comforting her alto voice singing *God is Love,*
what excitement she gave making Popsicle sticks
into disciples.

I remember how she believed in us girls,
how she kept us as long as she could. ❧

Butchers

Trying to become more organic, more kind,
responsible for my carbon footprint
I ask the neighbor girl to help me pick egg-laying
chicks from a catalogue.

We raise them in a cardboard box,
she knows each one by the color of down,
by beaks and feet,
teaches her sad-faced dog not to attack
after they are grown,
strutting their red capes around the yard.

None have died as I expected,
the coop too small for fifteen bantering hens.
So I hang a tin funnel from the clothesline,
snag a scratching pullet from the yard,
push her feathery breast down the funnel,
pull her head through the tiny hole.

She looks ridiculous upside down in her silver skirt,
squawking, waving her feet in the air.
With curious black-pebble eyes
she juts her head, up and down, left and right.

Holding a knife and a copy of *Mother Earth News*
my husband slits the jugular, careful
not to cut the esophagus or spine.

Across the field the girl comes running.
My head screams, *Go home, Go home.*
With newly cut hair and flowered jeans she stands
still as a mannequin next to the hanging bird
her mouth an *Oh*
as blood drips like a metronome to the bucket below.

I remember when I was her age,
watching death for the first time,
my cackling aunt in the yard
with a hatchet, placing a Buckeye Brown
on a stump, neck between two nails.

Inside our garage, over a gas burner,
a giant pot lid clangs as in a fairytale.
My husband hangs onto the hen's scaly legs
as the girl holds his wrist watch, timing a one-minute bath.
We pluck feathers by the handful,
place the pale puckered body in a tub of ice.

The girl walks home, slow,
two tears sliding down her apple cheeks.
Three days later she eats the chicken
with peas and mashed potatoes.

Finding my mother's recipe for chicken corn soup,
I recall her voice on the phone asking,
why chickens, you have a job and a supermarket.
I pull stubborn leftover feathers
her voice persists, *your father grew calluses*
converting the henhouse into a print shop.
I boil the meat off the bone,
those hockey tickets, church bulletins, wedding invitations,
put you through college.

Outside a hawk snatches an Araucana,
a mass of orange speckled feathers by the barn. ❧

Credits

In *Rhubarb*
"Beginnings," 1.3 (Summer 1999), 26.
"Yearnings," 8.15 (Fall 2007), 32-33.
"Resurrection," 21 (Spring 2009), 17.
"Things that Matter," 21 (Spring 2009), 18.
In *Mennonot*
"Beliefs," 8.15 (Fall 2007), 34.
In the *Mennonite Health Journal*
"Toil and Grace," 9.3 (July September 2007), 21.
In *Appalachian Heritage*
"Grantsville Stockyards," 35.1 (Winter 2007), 74-75.
In *The Hamilton Stone Review* online magazine issue 16
(Fall 2008)
"Butchers," "Shearing," "The Mennonite Relief Sale."
In *CMW Journal* online 1.6 (November 2009)
"Mother from Paradise," "Saving Maynard," "Into
Forever."
In *Wild Sweet Notes: Fifty Years of West Virginia Poetry 1950-
1999*. Ed. Barbara Smith and Kirk Judd. Huntington,
W.V.: Publishers Place, Inc., 2000.
"The Mennonite Relief Sale," 95-96 (an earlier version).
In *What Mennonites Are Thinking 2001*. Ed. Merle Good
and Phyllis Pellman Good. Intercourse, Pa.: Good
Books, 2001.
"What I Stole," 100-102.
In *Coal A Poetry Anthology*. Ed. Chris Green. Ashland, Ky.:
Blair Mountain Press, 2006.
"In Sago," 96-97.

In *Tongue Screws and Testimonies.* Ed. Kirsten Eve Beachy. Scottdale, Pa.: Herald Press, Pa., 2010. "Toil and Grace," 284-285.

My poem "Nickel Mines, PA, Oct. 2nd, 2006," won first place in The George Scarbrough Prize For Poetry, in the 2008 Mountain Heritage Literary Festival Writing Contest, Lincoln Memorial University. The judge was Lyrae Van Clief Stefanon, Academy of American Poets award-wining author of *Black Swan.*

My poem "Mother from Paradise" won first place in the West Virginia Writers long poetry division for 2009.

The Author

Cheryl Denise grew up in Elmira, Ontario. She earned a nursing degree at Conestoga College in Guelph, Ontario. For three years she worked as a volunteer through the Mennonite Church as a public health nurse in La Jara, Colorado. Now she and her husband live in the intentional community of Shepherds Field in West Virginia. The community raises Jacob sheep and a small flock of chickens. They produce and sell lambs, yarn, and soft, beautiful wool blankets. Cheryl works as a nurse supervisor for in-home care services for elderly and disabled persons.

Her poetry collection, *I Saw God Dancing* (DreamSeeker Books, 2005), was the winner of the 1998 West Virginia Writers Poetry Competition. Her poetry has appeared in various literary journals and publications, including the anthologies *Wild Sweet Notes: Fifty Years of West Virginia Poetry 1950-1999* (Publishers Place, Inc., 2000) and *Coal: A Poetry Anthology* (Blair Mountain Press, 2006).

CPSIA information can be obtained at www.ICGtesting.com
Printed in the USA
BVOW041924260412

288814BV00001B/5/P